Vital Teas & Soothing Tonics

Traditional and modern remedies that make you feel amazing

Rachel de Thample

Photography by Ali Allen

Kyle Books

Published in 2017 by Kyle Books
www.kylebooks.com

Distributed by National Book Network
4501 Forbes Blvd, Suite 200,
Lanham, MD 20706
Phone: (800) 462-6420
Fax: (800) 338-4550
customercare@nbnbooks.com

First published in Great Britain in 2017 by
Kyle Books, an imprint of Kyle Cathie Ltd

10 9 8 7 6 5 4 3 2 1

ISBN 978 1 909487 79 6

Editor: Judith Hannam
Editorial Assistant: Hannah Coughlin
Copy Editor: Anne McDowall
Nutritional Advice: Ciara Jean Roberts
Editorial Adaptation: Leda Scheintaub
Designer: Lucy Gowans
Photographer and Prop Stylist: Ali Allen
Food Stylist: Rachel de Thample
Illustrator: Laura Middleton
Production: Nic Jones and Gemma John

Library of Congress Control Number:
2017944846

Color reproduction by f1 color, London.
Printed and bound in China by C&C Offset
Printing Co., Ltd.

Important note: The information and advice contained in this book are intended as a
general guide and are not specific to individuals or their particular circumstances. Many
plant substances, whether sold as foods or as medicines and used externally or internally,
can cause an allergic reaction in some people. Neither the author nor the publishers can
be held responsible for claims arising from the inappropriate use of any remedy. Do
not attempt self-diagnosis or self-treatment for serious or long-term conditions before
consulting a medical professional or qualified practitioner. Do not undertake any self-
treatment while taking other prescribed drugs or receiving therapy without first seeking
professional guidance. Always seek medical advice if any symptoms persist.

Contents

Introduction

People around the world have been making tonics, teas, and tisanes for thousands of years as a way of keeping themselves healthy, energized, and nutritionally balanced. Many of these ancient remedies are as delicious as they are good for you, and for some time now I have incorporated them into my daily routine, under the guidance of nutritional therapist and friend Ciara Jean Roberts. As you will find if you do likewise, they will not only quench your thirst but also offer a whole range of nourishing and healing properties.

Simply starting your day with some turmeric in a Golden Chai (page 77) can reduce arthritic symptoms—I was getting achy joints, so I swapped it for my morning coffee and it truly made a difference. My mother had high blood pressure, which drinking Beet Kvass (page 27) almost instantly lowered. Whenever possible, choose organic ingredients, as they are free of pesticides and grown in soil that is rich with nutrients and minerals. Nonorganic soil is full of chemicals, meaning the chemicals are not only on your food but in it too. Second, filter your water or opt for mineral water that comes from a natural spring.

Most tap water is treated with chlorine, which counteracts many of the benefits and can kill off any fermented foods. Last, don't be tempted to use honey instead of sugar in the fermented recipes that call for sugar; the antibacterial qualities of honey will kill off your cultures. This is particularly important with water kefir and kombucha. Opt instead for organic raw, unrefined sugar. Or experiment with Palmyra jaggery, a traditional Ayurvedic sweetener that offers more nutritional value.

I've aimed to include a mix of drinks to give you a great variety to choose from. I hope you will find lots of opportunities to weave them into your day and to call upon them in times of need—whenever insomnia strikes or anxiety hits—or you just want a delicious nonalcoholic brew.

Here's to drinking to your health!

Using tonics and teas safely

The more one-on-one work I do, the more I come to understand that each person is unique and what works for one might not be so great for another. Plants contain powerful components that can work wonders for the human body. It is important, however, to realize that they need to be used with great respect. They contain chemicals that send signals to our cells, so they really do have an effect.

As you peruse the beautiful recipes Rachel has put together, ask yourself, "What calls to me?" "What is my medicine for today?" Choose your tonic or a tea according to your mood, and also consider the time of year. What is most seasonally appropriate for you? It might be that a simple mug of lemon juice in hot water is just the ticket or you might need something more therapeutic. The body is always changing, as is our mood, so see what sings to your cells on any given day.

The introduction of the right tonic or tea at the optimum time can make a life-changing difference. I had a client a few years ago who was in his early thirties and about to go onto heavy medication (methotrexate) for rheumatoid arthritis, which might have affected his fertility when he and his wife were looking to conceive a second child. I prescribed turmeric tea—simply a teaspoon of powder in warm water daily with breakfast—and this reduced his symptoms within just a few weeks. No meds were required, and he went on to have a beautiful baby girl.

It is important, however, to be mindful of what may or may not be appropriate for you. Many herbs should be avoided if you are pregnant or lactating, for example, while if you have any blood-sugar issues—if you are prediabetic or diabetic, for example—you should avoid recipes containing sugar. If you are taking medications, check for contraindications, and take particular care if you suffer from impaired kidney or liver function. If it feels wrong, don't do it. Learn to really tune in to your own body and its signals and how to best nourish yourself. Consider the therapeutic window of some of these offerings; administer a cough tonic as soon as you feel the onset of symptoms, for example. If you are taking a tea or tonic to help with a particular minor health complaint, do seek medical advice from a professional if the symptoms do not improve within a few days.

Fermentation is a growing trend, and there can be many benefits from including fermented foods and drinks in your diet. But if you are not accustomed to ferments, go easy and start with very small amounts, as they will influence the gut flora, which, if it has been out of balance, can take time to recalibrate.

Let these recipes inspire you, and be playful with them. The energy and intention you put into making them also has an effect on how they will resonate in your body. The ritual of making a tea or a tonic for yourself or for loved ones is all part of the process. I see much improvement in people struggling with sleep when they introduce a bedtime tea. I believe that this is a result not only of the combination of ingredients in the tea but also the act of taking time to create something beneficial for themselves. The more joy and open curiosity you can stir into your potion, the better!

Ciara Jean Roberts
NATUROPATHIC NUTRITIONAL THERAPIST AND YOGA TEACHER

Tonics

Seasonal ginger shots

Ginger truly does top the list of effective natural home remedies. Used throughout history around the world, ginger harnesses incredible healing power: not only does it help settle upset tummies and soothe migraines, but numerous studies suggest it can protect against cancer. Opt for organic where possible.

Below are my favorite ginger shot combos. Peel and juice the ginger first, then feed the herb or spice through the juicer and, finally, add the fruit. Each of the following makes 1 shot.

Asian pear drop

1 (¾-inch) piece fresh ginger, ¼ stalk lemongrass, and ½ pear

Persian ginger

1 (¾-inch) piece fresh ginger, 1 tablespoon fresh (unsprayed) rose petals or ¼ teaspoon rosewater, and 15 pitted cherries

Sunshine ginger

1 (¾-inch) piece fresh ginger, 1 blood orange or 2 clementines, and a dusting of cinnamon

Solo ginger

1 (¾-inch) piece fresh ginger, ¼ lemon (peel and all), and a dusting of cayenne pepper

Blushing ginger

1 (¾-inch) piece fresh ginger, 2 cardamom pods (feed them whole through your juicer or grind the seeds and add after juicing), 1½-inch piece of rhubarb, and 1 small or ½ medium beet

Winter ginger

1 (¾-inch) piece fresh ginger, 1 apple, 1 drop oregano essential oil (add the oregano after juicing)

Lime and cayenne shot

Doctors used to carry little jars of cayenne pepper with them in case of cardiac emergencies, as it has a powerful effect on circulation and blood pressure. Start with a small amount of cayenne, then slowly increase it.

Makes 1 shot

¼ teaspoon cayenne pepper

Juice of ½ lime

¼ cup water

½ teaspoon raw honey or maple syrup

In a glass, whisk the cayenne with the lime juice, top up with the water, then whisk in the honey or maple syrup.

Knock it back first thing in the morning, follow it with a glass of cold water, and feel your energy levels rise.

Charcoal shot

Activated charcoal is like a magnet for toxins and is used in emergency medicine in cases of accidental poisoning. It's great to clear your system. Take the activated charcoal tablet at night and drink the shot with a large glass of water upon waking, followed by lots of water during the day to assist with elimination.

Makes 1 shot

1 activated charcoal tablet

¼ cup fresh apple juice or pineapple juice (or water)

A squeeze of lime

½ teaspoon aloe vera (see page 21), or use bottled aloe vera juice

Take the charcoal tablet in the evening. In the morning, whisk the apple juice, lime juice, and aloe in a glass and drink immediately.

Turmeric shots

If you need a midmorning or afternoon energy boost, opt for one of these shots rather than a hit of espresso. It'll give you the sustained lift you need, while also delivering turmeric's numerous other health benefits.

Turmeric, pineapple, and black pepper shot
Juice 1 thumb-size piece each of peeled fresh turmeric and pineapple and add a pinch of finely ground black pepper.

Turmeric, carrot, and cayenne shot
Juice 1 thumb-size piece peeled fresh turmeric with 1 carrot. Finish with a squeeze of lemon or lime juice and a pinch of cayenne.

Turmeric, almond milk, and cardamom shot
This is like a smoothie shot. Blend 1 thumb-size piece peeled fresh turmeric with ½ cup almond milk or coconut milk and the ground seeds of 1 cardamom pod.

Lemon, lavender, and peppermint shot

Essential oils are concentrated plant power, and they can be hugely effective when applied in the right way for you and your unique constitution. Note that it is essential that you use food-grade essential oils, as other grades are not safe to ingest. The combo of lemon, lavender, and peppermint is immensely refreshing. I use it to clear sinus blockages, which I typically get after traveling. This is also a very soothing shot to take if you have a migraine. Admittedly, it tastes a bit unpleasant, but the effects, which are almost instant, make it worthwhile.

Makes 1 shot

2 drops lemon essential oil (food-grade)

2 drops peppermint essential oil (food-grade)

2 drops lavender essential oil (food-grade)

½ cup filtered or mineral water

Add the essential oil drops to a glass and top up with the water. Mix well, knock it back, and follow it with a fresh glass of water.

Repeat up to three times a day until symptoms subside. As always, if symptoms do not improve after a few days, seek medical advice.

Everyday health tonic

This tonic is a brilliant booster for every day health and a must-have remedy for flu season or when traveling overseas. The ginger helps to calm inflammation and create internal heat. The cayenne acts to boost circulation and horseradish is a decongestant. The garlic and onion help with overall immunity. Opt for fresh, organic ingredients to maximize benefits. If one of the ingredients is unavailable, simply double up on one of the other ingredients or just leave it out.

Makes 6 shots

2 tablespoons chopped garlic

2 tablespoons chopped onion

2 tablespoons grated fresh ginger

2 tablespoons grated fresh horseradish

2 tablespoons chopped cayenne chiles (or any seasonally available chiles)

1½ cups raw apple cider vinegar

Pile the garlic, onion, ginger, horseradish, and chiles into a 1-pint lidded jar. Pour in the vinegar, close the lid tightly, and shake.

Store at room temperature, but in a dark cool place. Shake at least once a day for two weeks. Then strain the tonic through a clean piece of cheesecloth, pour into a sterilized bottle, and label it. It will keep, at room temperature, for up to 6 months.

Take as soon as you feel symptoms of a cold in ¼-cup shots three times daily before eating. Avoid taking vinegar internally if you have a stomach ulcer.

How to sterilize jars
Wash jars and bottles in very hot, soapy water. Dry with a clean cloth then place in an oven, without the lids, at 210°F for 10 minutes. Bottling and sealing drinks while the liquid and container are still hot increases shelf life and decreases risk of spoilage.

Garlic and lemon elixir

This is an easy-to-make, all-round cleansing elixir. Garlic and lemon are a powerful antibacterial partnership. In clinical studies, garlic has been shown to significantly lower cholesterol, and in Germany, it is sometimes used for the treatment of atherosclerosis (hardening or blocking of the arteries). It has also long been used for the prevention of infections, colds, and flu. The whole lemon supports the immune system by having an alkalizing effect, while limonene, a compound found in the peel of citrus fruits, helps reduce inflammation.

Makes 21 shots

2 lemons

2 heads of garlic (or 20 cloves)

1 quart filtered or mineral water

Chop the lemons (peel and all) and garlic finely (or just blitz in a food processor).

Put the mixture into a medium saucepan, add the water, bring to a boil over medium-high heat, then reduce the heat and simmer for 15 minutes. Increase the heat and bring the mixture up to a rolling boil, then turn off the heat immediately and set aside to cool completely.

Once at room temperature, strain the liquid through a fine-mesh strainer set over a bowl, pressing on the solids to extract all the liquid. Discard the pulp and pour the liquid into sterilized bottles. Store the elixir in the fridge, where it will keep for up to 3 weeks.

Drink a shot (about ¼ cup) a day 2 hours before or after your main meal. Continue for 3 weeks. Take a break for a week, then make a new mix and repeat for an additional 3 weeks. At that time your whole body will feel regenerated!

Cough tonic

There are many potent ingredients here that create a powerful rejuvenating and soothing tonic to alleviate coughs. Use raw, cold-pressed honey as opposed to commercially heated honey to get the full nutritional and antibacterial benefits from it. The citrus juice adds vitamin C for a swifter recovery, while both ginger and turmeric have powerful anti-inflammatory properties.

Makes about 4 cups

¾ cup fresh oregano or thyme leaves (or a mixture)

1 (¾-inch) piece fresh ginger, peeled and grated

1 (¾-inch) piece fresh turmeric, peeled and grated

5 whole black peppercorns

2 cups filtered or mineral water

2 garlic cloves, grated

2 tablespoons raw honey or maple syrup

2 tablespoons fresh lime or lemon juice

Combine the oregano, ginger, turmeric, peppercorns, garlic, and water in a blender or high-powered food processor and blend until broken down (or roughly crush the dry ingredients in a mortar and pestle and then add the water). Pour into a medium saucepan, bring to a simmer, and simmer for 15 minutes.

Whisk in the honey or maple syrup and citrus juice to combine. Strain into a pitcher or large sterilized bottle though cheesecloth, pushing on the solids to squeeze out as much liquid as possible.

Drink a ½-cup mug of warmed cough tonic once or twice a day until your cough subsides. Sip slowly to allow the body to gently assimilate it.

Nettle tonic

Nettles are one of the most nutrient-dense wild foods that we have readily available to us. They have a good reputation as an iron tonic, as they not only contain relatively high levels of iron but also amino acids and vitamin C, both of which are required for iron absorption. If you are vegetarian or vegan, nettles are one of the best foods you can include in your diet for keeping your blood healthy. Nettles cause a stinging reaction when you touch them, so use gardening gloves when gathering them. Cooking removes their sting.

Serves 2

2 handfuls of nettles

4 apples, roughly chopped

½ lemon (peel and all), roughly chopped

6 sprigs of fresh mint

Place the nettles in a strainer and rinse well. Pour enough boiling water over the nettles to wilt them; this will deactivate their sting. Feed everything through a juicer, pour into a glass, and drink immediately.

Aloe cooler

Aloe vera is deeply soothing to the intestinal tissue, which makes this shot a great choice for digestive complaints. It also has a cooling effect, which can help mend internal scar tissue. It is used topically for burns. Drink once or twice a day (or simply take 1 to 2 tablespoons of aloe juice on its own) as a remedy or just because it's deliciously refreshing. Make sure the aloe juice is specified for internal consumption, or use fresh aloe leaves. You can find large aloe leaves from some natural food stores.

Makes about ¾ cup

1½-inch piece fresh, edible aloe (e.g. Aloe barbadensis) or 2 tablespoons aloe juice

¾ cup coconut water

Squeeze of lime

If you are using fresh aloe, wash it and place it on a plate flat-side up. Using a sharp knife, slice off the top rind, then cut it into 1½-inch cubes. Rinse the sticky coating from the clear flesh and freeze what you aren't using right away.

In a blender, blend the aloe flesh with the coconut water and add the lime juice. If you are using aloe juice, simply mix together all the ingredients. Pour into a glass and drink immediately.

Green juices

Wheatgrass and gooseberry

Wheatgrass juice contains a wealth of minerals and vitamins, making it an effective healer. It is also extremely rich in protein, and can regulate blood sugar, detoxify the liver, and so much more. Some even claim that it can keep your hair from turning gray! When gooseberries are out of season, swap in 4 apples and a squeeze of lime juice.

Serves 2

3 handfuls of fresh wheatgrass

8¾ ounces gooseberries

Feed the wheatgrass and gooseberries through a juicer. Pour into glasses and drink immediately.

Chlorella and coconut water

Ounce for ounce, chlorella, an algae, is more nutrient dense than broccoli and kale. It also contains high amounts of protein. Coconut water is very nourishing to the kidneys and helps prevent dehydration.

Serves 2

1 tablespoon chlorella powder

1¼ cups coconut water

In a glass, whisk the chlorella powder into the coconut water and drink immediately. Alternatively, add the powder to a bottle of coconut water, shake, and drink it on the go.

Apple and parsley juice

Fresh parsley contains high levels of both iron and vitamin C, making it good for blood health, especially if you are experiencing iron deficiency (anemia).

Serves 2

4 apples

¾ cup fresh parsley

½ lemon

Roughly chop all the ingredients and feed them through your juicer. Include all the bits of the lemon (zest, pith, and flesh) for maximum benefits. Pour into glasses and drink immediately.

Celery and cilantro juice

Celery can help to regulate levels of hydrochloric acid in the stomach. Cilantro is useful for heavy-metal detoxification and helps kill off intestinal parasites.

Serves 2

6 celery stalks

2 pears

⅔ cup fresh cilantro

½ lime, including peel

Roughly chop all the ingredients and feed them through your juicer. Pour into glasses and drink immediately.

Jamu kunyit

This ancient turmeric tonic is the Balinese equivalent to "an apple a day," as it is said to keep health problems at bay. Families in Bali have been brewing it up for more than five thousand years. They also call it the love potion, as it is believed to have an aphrodisiac effect. Try it and see...

Serves 4

4 thumb-size pieces fresh turmeric, peeled and grated

1 thumb-size piece fresh ginger, peeled and grated

1 tablespoon tamarind paste or the pulp from 2 whole tamarind pods

2 cups filtered or mineral water

2 to 3 tablespoons raw honey, maple syrup, or coconut palm sugar

Pinch of freshly ground black pepper (black or cubeb)

In a blender or food processor, combine the turmeric, ginger, and tamarind with the water and blend until smooth. Alternatively, pound everything to a paste, add the water, and let it infuse for 30 minutes.

Strain though a cheesecloth-lined strainer into a bowl, pressing on the solids to extract all the liquid. Add the honey and pepper. Drink immediately or transfer to a sterilized jar, cover, and place in the refrigerator, where it will keep for up to 1 week.

Beet kvass

A beautiful, blushing probiotic drink made with whey, a product that typically gets tossed yet is loaded with nutrients and is a useful source of amino acids. When you are sick and your appetite is low, you can supplement with whey to keep your protein intake up. Beets provide a wonderful boost of nitric oxide, which has a positive effect on the vascular system and arterial velocity. When making, keep the beet unpeeled, as the peel contains bacteria that helps kickstart fermentation. Just ensure you thoroughly wash them first.

Makes about 3 cups

2 medium beets, unpeeled, and cut into ¾- to 1¼-inch pieces

1 teaspoon sea salt or Himalayan pink salt

¼ cup whey or buttermilk

About 3 cups filtered or mineral water

Whey is a by-product of making cheese or labneh (strained yogurt), but buttermilk works just as well

Put the beets into 1-quart jar. Sprinkle the salt over the beets and add the whey.

Pour in the water, leaving a 2-inch gap at the top of the jar. Stir well. Loosely cover with the lid and leave in a cool, dark place for 2 to 5 days, until the kvass is effervescent. Transfer to the refrigerator. It will keep for 2 months.

Medicinal vinegars

Apple cider vinegar is one of the best kitchen remedies. It can help lower blood glucose, blood pressure, and bad cholesterol. Take 1 to 2 tablespoons daily (not more, as too much can be counterproductive). Opt for organic, raw cider vinegar, preferably with the mother.

Fill a sterilized jar about one-third full with your chosen herb, then pour in apple cider vinegar until the jar is full. Cover tightly and leave for 14 days in a cool, dark place, shaking well daily. Strain and pour into a sterilized bottle. Store in a cool, dark place for up to 1 year.

Rosemary	Useful for low energy and poor circulation, digestion, and nerves, and for increasing focus and concentration. Avoid daily use or if you're pregnant.
Sage	Antifungal, antibacterial, and antiviral. Avoiding using over an extended period of time or if you are pregnant or breast-feeding.
Thyme	Antiviral and antibacterial. Useful for upper respiratory infections, coughs, and bronchitis.
Oregano	Antiviral and antibacterial. Useful for upper respiratory infections.
Bee balm (Monarda)	Antibacterial, helpful for thick, congested coughs, sore throat, and fever.
Mint	Stomach-soothing digestive aid. Avoid if you have problems with your pyloric sphincter.
Rose petals	Astringent and anti-inflammatory. Medicine for the heart.
Elderflowers	Boosts the immune system. Useful for sore throats.
Black currant leaves	Packed with vitamin C, just like the fruit. Also, rich in antioxidants that have powerful anti-inflammatory properties.

Cherry Vanilla Shrub

I make all kinds of shrubs, also known as drinking vinegars, both as a refreshing healthy drink and to capture seasonal moments, especially in the summer, when juicy, sun-kissed fruits are in abundance. The easiest way to make these is without following a recipe. Just pile your fruit into a sterilized jar, cover with vinegar, and sweeten with honey or maple syrup to taste. You can add spices or herbs too, if you like. This particular version uses the classic combination of cherry and vanilla. To drink, simply strain the fruit out (you can eat it—try it in salads) and pour into a tumbler with ice. Top up with sparkling water or a good-quality tonic water. You can also add a shrub shot to a smoothie or use it to make virgin cocktails.

Makes 2 cups

2 cups fresh cherries, pitted

2 cups raw apple cider vinegar

2 to 3 tablespoons raw honey or maple syrup

½ vanilla pod

Ice cubes

Sparkling water

Put the pitted cherries in a sterilized jar, top up with the vinegar, add the honey and vanilla pod, then seal. Let sit at room temperature for 1 week or for up to 6 months in the fridge. The vinegar will preserve the fruit.

Strain into glasses over ice and top up with sparkling mineral water—roughly 1 part shrub to 2 parts sparkling water. Spoon a few cherries into the glasses (you can also use them in salads or other dishes).

Elderberry syrup with echinacea

Both elderberries and echinacea are powerful immune system boosters and have been used to prevent and treat colds and flu for many years. Ginger is also added to this syrup for its antimicrobial, antibiotic, and anti-inflammatory properties. This combo of immune powerhouses will give your nasty cold or flu a good beating!

Makes about 2½ cups

⅓ cup dried or ⅔ cup fresh elderberries

2 cups filtered or mineral water

¼ cup dried echinacea root or 1 teaspoon echinacea tincture

1 (1¼-inch) piece fresh ginger, peeled and thinly sliced

1 cinnamon stick

6 whole cloves

Zest and juice of 1 orange

⅓ cup raw honey

Put the elderberries and water into a saucepan along with the echinacea (if using the root), the ginger, cinnamon, cloves, and orange zest and juice. Bring to a rolling boil over high heat, then turn down the heat and simmer for 30 minutes, or until the consistency of maple syrup. It should be thick enough coat the back of spoon.

Leave to cool, then strain through a strainer lined with cheesecloth into a bowl, pressing on the solids to extract all the liquid. Whisk in the honey and the echinacea if you're using the tincture. Pour into sterilized bottles, cover, and store in the fridge for up to 3 months.

If you start to feel a cold or flu coming on—or even if you're just around someone who is sick—take once or twice throughout the day. If you do get sick, you can take a spoonful every couple of hours. Avoid taking it for more than a week or two at a time, however, as you need to give your body a break from the herbs to maximize the therapeutic window.

Rosehip syrup

Rosehip syrup is dripping with vitamin C and has long had a reputation for keeping colds at bay all winter. It has a surprisingly tropical tang, with notes of lychee and mango. Diluted with about five parts of cold water, it makes a delicious cordial drink that kids will love.

Makes about 1 cup

9 ounces fresh rosehips

1½ cups filtered or mineral water

⅓ cup raw honey or maple syrup

Roughly chop the rosehips in a food processor, then transfer to a saucepan and add the water. Bring to a boil over medium-high heat, then turn the heat down and simmer for 15 minutes.

Strain through a strainer lined with a double layer of cheesecloth, letting the pulp sit for at least 30 minutes so that all the juice passes through. Press with a wooden spoon to squeeze out as much liquid as possible.

Gently heat the extracted juice until just warmed through, then remove from the heat and whisk in the honey or maple syrup.

Pour the syrup into a sterilized bottle or jar while it's still hot. Cool, then seal and use within 3 months. Refrigerate once opened. Take 1 to 2 tablespoons daily to help keep colds at bay.

Dandelion and burdock cordial

Dandelion is a useful liver tonic, as it helps to increase the flow of bile, which is important in the digestive process for the breakdown of fat and the removal of waste products. Burdock is a blood purifier and lymph cleanser. It also contains the fiber inulin, which helps to bulk the stool to make you more regular. Wood avens is a beautiful plant with roots that impart a cinnamon-like flavor. You can use fresh or dried roots for this recipe, or, if unavailable, substitute a cinnamon stick. You can dig up fresh roots from your garden— just be sure you know what you're looking for—or order dried roots online (see page 92 for suppliers).

Makes 1¾ cups

½ ounce wood avens roots, thoroughly cleaned, or 1 cinnamon stick

1¾ ounces dandelion roots

1¾ ounces burdock root

1 thumb-size piece fresh ginger, peeled and chopped

12 whole cloves

3 cups filtered or mineral water

⅓ cup maple syrup

If using fresh roots, clean them thoroughly before roughly chopping.

Place all the ingredients except the maple syrup in a small saucepan, bring to a boil, and boil for 15 minutes. Strain into a clean jug. Whisk in the maple syrup.

Cool, then transfer to a jar or bottle, cover, and keep in the fridge for up to 2 weeks. Serve topped up with chilled soda water.

Brain booster

Brahmi, used in this tonic, is named after the Hindu God Brahma, believed to be the all-pervading consciousness responsible for all creative forces in the world. Brahmi is traditionally known as a nerve tonic, soothing anxiety and tension, calming the mind and body, and promoting relaxation. It is beneficial for promoting mental clarity, alertness, and short- and long-term memory, while relieving mental fatigue. It is mild and gentle, and safe for children and adults alike.

Serves 2

¾ cup walnuts

3 pitted dates

1 teaspoon vanilla extract or seeds from ½ vanilla pod

½ tablespoon ground cinnamon

2 teaspoons brahmi mushroom extract

Place everything in a high-speed blender and whizz together, slowly adding 2 cups filtered or mineral water through the feed tube until the ingredients are broken down.

For a smoother consistency, strain through a fine-mesh strainer or cheesecloth into a pitcher. Drink immediately or chill until ready to drink. Will keep 2 days in the refrigerator.

Milk kefir

Kefir originated in parts of Eastern Europe and Southwest Asia. The name is derived from the Turkish word keyif, which means "feeling good" after eating. Kefir contains about thirty different microorganisms, making it a much more potent source of probiotics than other fermented dairy products. The nutritional content of kefir will vary depending on the milk quality and length of fermentation. Kefir is high in vitamin B12, an important nutrient for the nervous system.

Makes 2½ cups

2½ cups whole cow's milk, coconut milk, or almond milk (see Note)

1 tablespoon milk kefir grains

1 dried fig, quartered (optional)

Dusting of cinnamon (optional)

For best results, if using cow's milk, opt for organic—even better if it's unhomogenized or raw. If using almond milk, blend with two dates, strain, and then add the grains—the grains need sugars to feed them, which cow's milk and coconut milk have naturally.

Mix the milk and kefir grains in a sterilized 1-quart jar. Add the dried fig, if using—it will help speed up fermentation and adds a lovely flavor.

Cover the jar with a clean kitchen towel and leave in a warm place for 12 to 24 hours, until it thickens and is slightly tangy and fizzy. Strain into a jar and store in the fridge until you're ready to drink it. Sprinkle with cinnamon before serving. Kefir is best enjoyed within 2 weeks; it will continue to ferment as you keep it in the fridge.

STORING MILK KEFIR GRAINS
When you're not making a new batch of kefir, store them covered in milk in a jar in the fridge.

Water kefir

Water kefir has been around for hundreds of years. In the late 1800s, the grains were used in Mexico to ferment a drink made from the sweetened juice of the prickly pear cactus. Other documentation traces their use to Tibet, the Caucasus Mountains, and the southern peninsula of Ukraine. The benefits are similar to dairy-based kefir—the grains contain more than thirty strains of beneficial bacteria—making this a great alternative to dairy products.

Makes 4 x 1-cup servings

3 tablespoons unrefined sugar

4 cups filtered water, bottled water, or coconut water

2 tablespoons water kefir grains

2 tablespoons mixed fruit such as dried mango, dried sour cherries, or dried fig

2 slices of lemon, lime or orange (optional)

In a sterilized 1½-quart jar, whisk the sugar and water together until the sugar dissolves. Add the kefir grains and the dried fruit and citrus slices, if using.

Cover with a clean kitchen towel or double layer of cheesecloth. Set aside in a cool, dark place to ferment for 2 days. The kefir should have a mild apple cider vinegar tang to it and have the fizz of sparkling water. Strain the kefir grains through a nylon strainer or a colander lined with a cheesecloth (avoid metal, as it can deactivate the grains).

Pour the kefir into a container and refrigerate until ready to drink. It will keep in the fridge for up to 3 weeks.

REUSING KEFIR GRAINS
Keep using the kefir grains, or store them in the fridge in brewed water kefir from your last batch to cover for up to 2 weeks between batches. They need to be fed as least every 2 weeks to keep their potency.

Tropical detox smoothie

Papaya seeds, pumpkin seeds, and cloves are all hugely effective in getting rid of intestinal parasites and are all-round digestive cleansers. Pineapple has many benefits thanks to its powerful enzyme, bromelain, which acts to help break down food and aid nutrient assimilation. It is also helpful for countering allergies and sinusitis. The highest bromelain content is found in the core of the pineapple, so be sure to use that part too. This smoothie is particularly good to drink while recovering from surgery and injuries.

Serves 2

½ papaya (with the black seeds), peeled and chopped

¼ pineapple, peeled

4 whole cloves, freshly ground

2 tablespoons coconut oil

2 tablespoons grated coconut

2 tablespoons pumpkin seeds (soaked in water to cover overnight then drained if possible)

2 cups coconut water

In a blender, combine all the ingredients and blend until as smooth as possible—it will be quite textured. Add a little more coconut water, if needed to thin. Drink immediately.

Teas

Loose-leaf teas

The world of tea is vast and can easily be likened to the world of wine. Like wine, there are so many different terroirs that lend to a tea's unique profile. When tea is picked, which part of the plant is harvested and how it is processed afterward all play a part in determining its flavor. And that's just focussing on camellia sinensis, the plant from which tea is made.

Looking at tisanes made from herbs, spices, and flowers opens up a whole other world of flavors to tantalize the taste buds, and strengthen body and mind. There is such a wonderful array of herbal, Ayurvedic, and other alternative teas available these days. Buying a few basics (see page 92) and brewing up your own tea blends is often cheaper, fresher, more flavorful, and more fun than buying them—and they make wonderful gifts too.

How to make your own tea bags

Buy unbleached cheesecloth—either a whole roll or individual pieces—and cut into small squares (about 3 inches). Fill each square of material with 1 tablespoon loose-leaf tea (more or less, depending on the blend). Ensure there is enough space for the tea leaves to move around once tied. Secure with kitchen string.

If you want to compost the teabags, make sure the fabric and string are fully compostable. Alternatively, buy ready-to-fill tea bags online. Opt for unbleached varieties, as bleach is not good for you and would cancel out the benefits of a beautiful homemade tea or tisane blend.

Jasmine tea	Regarded in Chinese medicine as an herb with balanced character, jasmine flowers—used to scent tea—can relieve the blood vessels around your eyes and help relax your muscles, making it a good choice to enjoy after a long day of work. Brew 2 tablespoons of leaves with 3 tablespoons cold water, topped up with 1 cup freshly boiled water. Steep for 3 minutes. Infuse two or three more times. The mix of hot and cold water gives a more full bodied tea.
White tea	White teas are the least processed of all teas, with fresh spring flower, melon, cucumber, and honey flavors. They are reputed for helping maintain healthy, youthful skin. Silver Needle (pictured), the most famous white tea, is composed only of young leaf buds. Brew 2 tablespoons leaves with 3 tablespoons cold water, topped up with 1 cup freshly boiled water. Steep for 3 minutes. Infuse two or three more times.
Green tea	From China's expertly fired Dragon Well and the exuberant flavors of Anji Green to the delicately vegetal character of the steamed or shaded green teas of Japan, such as Gyokuro (pictured), green teas cover a broad spectrum of flavors. Leaves are picked at the beginning of spring and are energy dense with a bundle of health benefits: lowering the risk of cancer and reducing cholesterol, for example. Brew 1 heaping tablespoon of leaves with 2 to 3 tablespoons cold water, topped up with 1 cup freshly boiled water. Steep for 3 minutes. Infuse two or three more times.
Oolong tea	Complex flavors in oolong teas come from repeated stages of oxidation, shaping, and firing. They're often highly aromatic, with floral and toasty flavors. Oolongs are great antioxidants and can protect against tooth decay. Brew 1 heaping tablespoon with 1 cup freshly boiled water. Steep for 5 minutes. Infuse two or three more times.
Pu-erh tea	Pu-erh teas are highly revered in China, where the processing methods have remained a well-guarded secret for centuries. The tea is fermented before being aged and is packed into bricks. The careful ageing process adds a fascinating dimension to the flavor, maturing the tea into something richer, smoother, mellower, and more complex without losing the original life of the young fresh leaf. Pu-erh is great for settling the digestive system after a heavy meal and is also said to aid in weight loss. Brew 1 heaping teaspoon or 1 mini pu-erh cake with ⅔ cup freshly boiled water. Steep for 7 minutes. Infuse two or three more times.
Olive leaf tea	Olive leaves have been consumed throughout history—in powdered form, tinctures, and as a tea. They contain compounds with antioxidant and anti-inflammatory properties, with their nutritional value similar to that of a good-quality olive oil. You can dry olive tree leaves to make your own tea. Brew 1 tablespoon with 1 cup freshly boiled water for 10 minutes.

Detox teas

Lemon verbena and calendula tea

Lemon verbena and calendula are soothing to the gut. Calendula contains high amounts of flavonoids to help relax muscles and increase blood flow, which relieves menstrual cramps. Lemon verbena is a soothing partner and has been shown to increase white blood cells, making it a boost for the immune system.

Serves 1

2 tablespoons fresh or dried lemon verbena

1 teaspoon dried or 1 tablespoon fresh calendula petals

1¼ cups freshly boiled water

Add the lemon verbena and calendula to a teapot and pour over the freshly boiled water. Steep for 10 minutes then strain into a mug. Drink warm, or chill and drink cold.

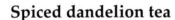

Spiced dandelion tea

This rich, earthy brew is more like a light coffee and is packed with ingredients to make you glow. Dandelion roots have a diuretic action that helps cleanse the body without depleting it. Star anise helps clear the digestive system, as does cardamom, which also reduces toxins in the blood and skin. Licorice can help manage negative the effects of excessive adrenaline and is anti-inflammatory, helping the skin inside and out.

Serves 1

1 tablespoon dried dandelion root

1 star anise pod

3 cardamom pods

½ dried licorice root or 1 teaspoon shredded dried licorice root

1¼ cups freshly boiled water

Place all the ingredients in a teapot and pour over the freshly boiled water. Steep for 15 minutes, then strain into a mug and drink.

Elderflower and lemon tea

The distinctive lacy blooms of the elderflower have been used medicinally for more than four thousand years in a number of cultures for their anti-inflammatory and antiseptic properties. Elderflower is rich in flavonoids, including quercetin, which give it the ability to calm systemic inflammation. The vibrant combination of elderflower with fresh lemon is one to lift the spirits.

Serves 1

A slice of lemon

1 tablespoon dried elderflower (see Note)

1 cup freshly boiled water

* Use fresh elderflowers when they are in season—substitute 2 tablespoons fresh for the dried. You can dry the fresh flowers so you can enjoy this tea all year round.

Bundle the slice of lemon and elderflower into a teapot. Cover with the freshly boiled water and top up with ½ cup cold water. Steep for 5 minutes, then strain into a mug and drink.

Chicory chai

The inulin in chicory root also acts as a prebiotic fiber because it's highly fermentable when it reacts with the friendly bacteria in the gut. Prebiotics can help promote the growth of probiotics in your digestive system and may enhance calcium absorption. This is why you're likely to see chicory root fiber in probiotic supplements. The classic mix of chai spices gives it an added boost, as these warming ingredients are great for digestive health.

Serves 1

2 tablespoons chicory coffee powder

½ cinnamon stick or ¼ teaspoon ground cinnamon

6 whole cloves

4 black peppercorns

A grating of nutmeg

1 (¼-inch) slice fresh ginger, peeled

3 crushed cardamom pods

1¼ cups coconut milk, almond milk, or hazelnut milk

A drop of raw honey or maple syrup (optional)

Place all the ingredients except the honey in a small saucepan and bring to a simmer over medium heat. Reduce the heat and simmer for 15 to 20 minutes.

Strain out the spices and serve warm. To speed things up, use a coffee grinder to grind all the spices to a powder and reduce the simmering time to 5 minutes.

Strain and serve. Sweeten with a drop of honey if you like.

VARIATIONS
Chocolate Chai: *Replace the chicory powder with raw cacao powder.*
Rooibos Chai: *Replace the chicory powder with loose rooibos tea leaves or two rooibos tea bags.*
Chai Coffee: *Replace the chicory powder with ¾ cup freshly brewed coffee and reduce the milk to ½ cup.*

Citrus wake-up calls

As simple as it seems, starting your day with a mug of hot water with lemon really makes a difference to your health. It is a fabulous way to hydrate after the long hours of sleep, and it helps to freshen up the whole system. Lemon will gently stimulate the liver, and drinking it in warm water is best, as cold water requires the body to expend more energy. If you want a little twist to your morning citrus routine, try one of the following brews, which have additional health benefits.

Morning sunshine

Serves 1

2 clementines

1¼-inch piece fresh ginger, peeled and thinly sliced

1 small fresh turmeric root, peeled and thinly sliced

1 cup freshly boiled water

Clementines and ginger contain lots of vitamin C, which is good for skin. There's plenty of orange color here, indicating the presence of carotenes, which are good for eye health. Ginger and turmeric together create a strong anti-inflammatory action.

Halve the clementines and squeeze the juice into a teapot. Add the squeezed fruit along with the ginger and turmeric to the teapot. Pour over the freshly boiled water, steep for 5 minutes or longer, then strain into a mug and drink.

Sicilian garden tea

Serves 1

1 lemon

2 rosemary sprigs

1 cinnamon stick

1 cup freshly boiled water

Aromatic rosemary has an uplifting and invigorating effect, and cinnamon helps to balance blood sugar levels. This tea makes for a great start to the day and is a lovely twist on classic lemon tea.

Strip the lemon zest using a vegetable peeler and put it into a teapot, then squeeze the juice into the teapot. Add the rosemary and cinnamon and pour over the freshly boiled water. Steep for 5 minutes, then strain into a mug and drink.

Cozy bedtime tea

The ritual of making a bedtime tea can be enough to calm the mind. Chamomile and lavender soothe the nervous system and tone the parasympathetic nervous system, stimulating our "rest-and-digest" mode—the ideal state before bed. Chamomile also helps to reduce excess cortisol, a stress hormone that can be damaging in large amounts. Chamomile can ease stomach cramps and may also be helpful in preventing migraines. Take twice a day to ease menstrual cramping. Use with caution or avoid altogether if you are pregnant or attempting to conceive.

Serves 1

2 teaspoons dried chamomile flowers

1 teaspoon dried lavender flowers

A grating of nutmeg

1 cup freshly boiled water

Combine the chamomile, lavender, and nutmeg in a teapot and pour over the freshly boiled water. Steep for 5 minutes, then strain into a mug and drink.

Sweet dreams

This combination is a wonderful tea for the nervous system. Lemon balm is useful for soothing an upset stomach. Be mindful if you are hypothyroid, as lemon balm can inhibit thyroid function (this is not an issue for those with healthy thyroid function).

Serves 1

1 tablespoon fresh or dried lemon balm leaves

2 teaspoon dried lime flowers or 2 tablespoons fresh lime flowers

1 teaspoon dried rose buds or 1 tablespoon fresh rose petals

1 cup freshly boiled water

Put the lemon balm, lime flowers, and rose buds into a teapot and pour over the freshly boiled water. Top up with ¼ cup cold water. Steep for 10 minutes, then strain into a mug and drink.

Grasshopper tea

The amino acid L-theanine in green tea helps to promote a calm alertness, while mint adds an uplifting aroma and also helps to freshen the breath. This is a great drink when you're in need of some clarity and focus. This tea can be taken regularly—so embrace your inner grasshopper!

Serves 1

2 teaspoons green tea leaves or 1 green tea bag

Large handful of fresh mint or 1 peppermint tea bag

1 cup freshly boiled water

Place the green tea and mint in a teapot. Pour over the freshly boiled water and top up with ½ cup cold water. Steep for 5 minutes, then strain into a mug and drink.

Nettle and mint tea

Nettles are a great kidney cleanser and can reduce kidney inflammation (nephritis) and act as a mild diuretic. If you can, forage fresh nettles for this energizing tea. If you encounter an abundance of them, gather extra to dry for later in the year. Note that nettles cause a stinging reaction when you touch them, so use gardening gloves when gathering them. Cooking removes the sting.

Serves 1

15 fresh nettle leaves or 1 teaspoon dried nettle leaves

2 sprigs fresh mint or 1 teaspoon dried peppermint

1 cup freshly boiled water

If you are using fresh nettles, rinse them to remove any soil or grit. Place the fresh or dried leaves in a teapot along with the mint. Pour over the boiling water, followed by ½ cup cold water. Steep for 10 minutes, then strain into mugs and drink warm, or refrigerate and drink cold.

Scarborough fair tea

With a quartet of healing herbs—rosemary for concentration, thyme to soothe respiratory issues, parsley for its iron content, and sage to nourish a sore throat—this is a wonderful winter brew to stave off colds and other bugs.

Serves 1

2 sprigs fresh rosemary

2 sprigs fresh thyme

3 fresh sage leaves

1 large sprig fresh parsley

1 cup freshly boiled water

Pile the fresh herbs into a teapot. Pour over the freshly boiled water and top up with ¼ cup cold water. Steep for 7 minutes, then strain into a mug and drink.

Holy basil tea

Also known as tulsi, holy basil is nutritive to the adrenal glands, making this tea helpful for those suffering from adrenal fatigue. It also helps reduce levels of cortisol, a stress hormone produced by the adrenal glands, making it useful for combatting anxiety and cortisol-driven weight gain.

Serves 1

1 tablespoon fresh holy basil leaves

½ teaspoon chopped lemongrass or ginger, or ½ cinnamon stick

1 cup freshly boiled water

In a teapot, combine all the ingredients, cover, and leave for 5 minutes to steep.

Strain into tea cups and drink warm, or chill and serve over ice.

Good digestion teas

Zen tea

There's plenty of digestive loveliness in this recipe!
Sip it a little at a time, as it contains a powerhouse
of ingredients that the body needs to absorb slowly.

Serves 2

3 (¼-inch) slices fresh ginger

1 tablespoon dried peppermint
or 6 sprigs fresh peppermint

¼ teaspoon caraway seeds

¼ teaspoon fennel seeds

¼ teaspoon coriander seeds

1 star anise pod

2 cups freshly boiled water

Add the herbs and spices to a teapot and pour over the
freshly boiled water. Steep for 5 to 10 minutes.

Strain into mugs and serve.

Tummy soother

Fennel is used widely in Ayurvedic medicine for digestive
issues. It can occasionally cause nausea, so start with a little
and build up. People with uncontrolled high blood pressure
should avoid licorice.

Serves 2

1 tablespoon dried peppermint

6 whole cloves

1 teaspoon fennel seeds

½ licorice root

2 cups freshly boiled water

Add the peppermint, cloves, and fennel seeds to a teapot.
Crush or snap the licorice root a little and add it too. Pour
over the freshly boiled water, steep for 5 to 10 minutes,
then strain into mugs and drink.

Women's balance tea

This is a luxurious, calming, and soothing tea to help ease fluctuations in women's monthly cycle. Sipping tea made with rose petals can help alleviate heavy bleeding. Here they're paired with saffron and raspberry leaves, which are both known to help relieve menstrual pain. The vanilla is there to sweeten and soothe. If you can find shatavari powder (see page 192 for online resources), do include it, but if you can't get hold of it, the tea is delicious and beneficial without. Shatavari is a species of asparagus, and the powdered root makes a wonderful tonic for women to help nourish the reproductive system. But men can enjoy this tea too!

Serves 1

1 teaspoon dried raspberry leaves

1 tablespoon dried rose petals or buds

Pinch of saffron threads

1 (¾-inch) slice vanilla pod (optional)

½ teaspoon shatavari root powder

1¼ cups freshly boiled water

Put the raspberry leaves, rose petals, saffron, vanilla, and shatavari, if using, into a teapot and pour over the freshly boiled water. Steep for 10 minutes, then strain into a mug and serve.

Vietnamese lemongrass tea

Lemongrass is effective for taming achy tummies.
The lemonal compound contained in lemongrass makes
it a mild astringent and antiseptic, and it's also great for
soothing coughs and keeping colds and flu at bay.

Serves 2

2½ cups filtered or mineral water

4 lemongrass stalks

1 thumb-size piece fresh ginger

1 tablespoon coconut sugar or raw honey, or to taste

Lime slices (optional)

In a medium saucepan, bring the water to a boil over high heat. Smash the lemongrass and cut it into thin shreds. Peel and julienne the ginger. Add both to the water and boil for 5 minutes.

Reduce the heat to low and simmer for an additional 5 minutes.

Add the coconut sugar or honey, to taste, and serve warm with a garnish of lime slices if you like, or refrigerate and serve over ice.

Tom yum tea

A brilliant cold-busting tea that tastes a bit like tom yum soup. Take two to three times daily when you feel a cold coming on, but avoid drinking it late at night, as the ginger and cayenne make this quite a stimulating tea.

Serves 1

1 lemon

1 garlic clove

1 (¾-inch) piece fresh ginger

Pinch of cayenne pepper

1 cup freshly boiled water

½ to 1 teaspoon raw honey or maple syrup

Strip the lemon zest using a vegetable peeler and put it into a mug. Squeeze in the juice, straining out the pits. Peel and grate or crush the garlic straight into the mug. Peel and grate in the ginger into the mug and add the cayenne.

Pour over the freshly boiled water and steep for 5 to 10 minutes.

Sweeten with the honey, stir, and drink.

Armenian herbal tea

The Armenian highlands, located in the mountainous region between the Black and Caspian Seas, host pristine alpine habitats that produce an abundance of wild herbs. There a blend of wild mountain thyme and linden flowers (also known as lime flowers) is widely sipped for both its flavor and nourishing qualities. Forage lime flowers in spring, order them online, or buy from a store that sells dried herbs.

Serves 1

6 sprigs fresh thyme

1 teaspoon fresh or dried lime flowers

Strip of fresh orange zest (optional)

1 cup freshly boiled water

Put the thyme, lime flowers, and orange zest, if using, in a teapot and pour over the freshly boiled water. Steep for 5 minutes, then strain into a mug and drink.

Spice route teas

Saffron and cardamom tea

An elegant blend of spices and green tea, this brew packs a health punch. Studies in India suggest that cardamom may be helpful in cases of colorectal cancer, while saffron is rich in crocin, a carotene that helps to keep cells healthy.

Serves 1

4 cardamom pods

Pinch of saffron

2 teaspoons green tea leaves or 1 green tea bag

1 cup freshly boiled water

Roughly crush the cardamom pods and put both the green husks and the black seeds in a teapot along with the saffron and tea leaves. Pour in the freshly boiled water and top up with ¼ cup cold water. Steep for 7 minutes, then strain into a mug and drink.

Spice C tea

Cumin is a wonderful cleanser for the small intestine, which plays an important role in nutrient absorption. You may be eating the best food, but if your ability to absorb and assimilate the nutrients is diminished, your health will be affected. If this is the case, try this tea for one month.

Serves 1

1 teaspoon cumin seeds

½ cinnamon stick

2 teaspoons black tea leaves or 1 black tea bag

1 cup freshly boiled water

Put the cumin, cinnamon, and tea leaves into a teapot and pour over the freshly boiled water. Steep for 7 minutes, then strain into a mug.

Rosy ginger tea

Rose works to calm the emotions, making it a medicine for your heart, while ginger and star anise are great digestive soothers.

Serves 1

1 (1¼-inch) piece fresh ginger, peeled and roughly chopped

1 tablespoon rose petals or buds

1 star anise pod

1 cup freshly boiled water

Put the ginger, rose petals, and star anise into a teapot and pour over the freshly boiled water. Steep for 10 minutes, then strain into a mug and drink.

Afghan pink chai

This intriguing traditional Afghan drink, also known as Qaimaq or Sheer chai, is often served at celebrations to toast good health. The addition of baking soda is what magically turns the green tea–based drink pink (I add a little beet juice to further the effect). Baking soda is helpful for maintaining the acid-alkaline balance in the body.

Serves 2

1 tablespoon green tea leaves or green tea bag

⅛ teaspoon baking soda

2 cups cow's milk (preferably organic or raw) or almond milk

Seeds from 6 cardamom pods, roughly crushed

1 cinnamon stick

10 whole cloves

1 teaspoon beet juice or powdered beets (optional)

1 to 2 teaspoons raw honey or coconut palm sugar, to taste (optional)

Place everything, apart from the beet juice and honey or sugar, into a saucepan. Bring to a rapid boil for 1 minute.

Turn off the heat and let steep for 15 minutes. It should be a pale shade of pink. For added blush, whisk in a little beet juice or powdered beet, if you like.

Strain the spices from the drink and sweeten to taste. Serve warm.

Vanilla and nutmeg matcha latte

Unlike other green tea leaves that are steeped then strained, with matcha tea you're actually consuming dried and powdered leaves, which means this tea is packed with antioxidants and offers a sustained energy boost. It's a great alternative to coffee, as it gives you a caffeine buzz without the subsequent crash.

Serves 1

1 cup almond milk

Drop of vanilla extract (less than ⅛ teaspoon) or a small scraping of vanilla seeds (less than ¼ pod)

Pinch of freshly grated nutmeg

1 teaspoon matcha tea powder

½ to 1 teaspoon raw honey or maple syrup

In a small saucepan, gently warm the milk with the vanilla and nutmeg. Increase the temperature to achieve a soft, rolling boil, then immediately remove from the heat.

Whisk in the matcha powder until frothy. Add the honey and serve warm or, in warm weather, you can simply whisk all the ingredients together and serve cold.

Drinks

Golden lassi

The anti-inflammatory action of turmeric combined with mineral-rich banana or mango make this a good drink for muscle recovery after a workout.

Serves 2

1 thumb-size piece fresh turmeric or 1 teaspoon ground turmeric

2 ripe bananas or 1 small to medium ripe mango

2 cups natural yogurt or dairy kefir

Peel and roughly chop the turmeric, bananas or mango (if using mango also pit it). Transfer the fruit to blender or food-processor, along with the yogurt or kefir, and blend until smooth.

Trickle in a little water to thin, if needed. Drink straight away or chill and drink within 24 hours.

Frothy ayran

Originating from Turkey, this hydrating yogurt drink is made for the summer months, and the added salt helps replace natural salts lost through sweating. It's traditionally taken as an antidote to spicy foods, so serve it to cool down your favorite spicy dishes.

Serves 2

⅔ cup plain whole-milk yogurt

Pinch of sea salt

1½ cups sparkling water

Ice cubes

Fresh mint sprigs or dried mint

Put the yogurt and salt in a blender or large bowl and blend or whisk the sparkling water in little by little, until frothy and well mixed. Pour into glasses over ice and garnish with a fresh mint sprigs or a sprinkling of dried mint.

Nut, seed, and grain milks

You can blend pretty much any seed, nut, or grain with water, strain, and it produces a brilliant milk alternative. The benefits of substituting plant-based milks for dairy is that they're easier to digest and contain a wide array of nutrients, especially if you make them with a combination of nuts, seeds, and grains.

Basics

Makes 2 cups

3½ ounces nuts, seeds, or grains

1 to 2 pitted dates (optional)

3½ cups filtered or mineral water

Place the nuts, seeds, or grains in a bowl and add the dates, if using. Top with water to cover by a couple inches. Cover and soak in the fridge for 12 hours or overnight.

Drain and rinse, then transfer to a blender, add the water, and blend until smooth. Strain, squeezing out as much liquid out as possible, and store in the fridge for up to 5 days.

Milk combos

Almond and mixed seed milk
Sunflower, sesame, and pumpkin seeds are a delicious and nutritious addition. Opt for a 50-50 mix of almonds and seeds and use in any recipe in place of almond milk.

Hemp seed milk
Delicious on its own or go 50-50 with almonds or cashews. Hemp milk is delicious blended with a date or two, a drop of vanilla extract, and 1 teaspoon ground cinnamon.

Oat milk
Perfect in banana-based smoothies, or warmed with honey and nutmeg for a soothing bedtime drink. Note that rolled oats don't need to be soaked (steel-cut oats do).

Cashew milk
This is the thickest, creamiest, and most milk-like of all and is perfect cold with a dusting of cinnamon.

Hazelnut milk
This is one of my favorite milks and is delicious in the Chicory Chai on page 50 or in the Aztec Hot Chocolate on page 79.

Coconut milk

Fresh coconut milk is rich in antioxidants and will give your immune system a boost. It also acts as a muscle relaxant because of its high mineral content, and it is antibacterial. Half the fat found in coconut is a type called lauric acid. The body converts lauric acid to monolaurin, which acts to destroy viruses and gram-negative bacteria. The medium-chain fatty acids found in coconut oil and coconut milk are easily digested and go straight to the liver to be used for energy.

Makes about 3 cups

1 fresh mature coconut

About 3 cups filtered or mineral water

Crack your coconut open: Wrap the coconut in cheesecloth, then set it in a metal bowl and bang it with a mallet or hammer. Use the cheesecloth to strain the water away from the coconut and into a new bowl.

Carefully pry the flesh from the shell using a knife and roughly chop it. Put the flesh into a blender or food processor and start blending, adding the reserved coconut water and then the filtered water, a little at a time through the hole in the lid, until the coconut flesh is as fine as grated coconut and the liquid is thick and creamy. Add more or less water depending on the size of your coconut and how thick and creamy you want it.

Use a cheesecloth to strain the coconut milk, reserving the pulp for use in salads, or dry it to make your own shredded coconut. It will keep in the fridge for 2 to 3 days, or freeze it for up to 6 months and defrost in the fridge when needed.

Golden chai

Serves 1

1 cup almond milk

2 small or 1 large fresh turmeric root, peeled and roughly chopped

Seeds from 2 cardamom pods

Pinch of freshly ground black pepper

1 teaspoon coconut oil

1 teaspoon raw honey or maple syrup, or to taste

Turmeric has been widely researched, with its active compound curcumin believed to provide a plethora of benefits, including modulation of gene expression, reduction of inflammation, protection against liver damage, enhanced wound healing, and suppression of tumor formation. Turmeric is a wonderful addition to our daily diet. This recipe can easily be scaled up.

In a blender, combine all the ingredients and blend until smooth. Drink cold or warm. It will keep, refrigerated, for up to 1 week.

If you wish to make a large batch to drink throughout the week, it will keep in the fridge for up to 4–5 days.

Ruby latte

Serves 1

1 cup almond milk or coconut milk

2 tablespoons beet juice or 1 tablespoon beet powder

Pinch of ground cinnamon

¼ teaspoon vanilla bean seeds or extract

1 (¼-inch) slice fresh ginger

Seeds from 2 cardamom pods, ground (optional)

This beet-based latte is part of a growing range of superfood lattes. It features beet juice or powder, a plant-based milk, and a blend of spice. It's hugely satisfying and, unlike coffee, will lower blood pressure.

In a small saucepan, combine all the ingredients, place over medium heat, and whisk until frothy and warmed through. Serve immediately, or cool, store in a jar in the fridge, and warm it up in the morning.

Butter-froth coffee

Serves 2

¼ cup freshly ground organic coffee beans

2 cups freshly boiled water

¼ cup cold water

2 tablespoons grass-fed butter or ghee

2 tablespoons coconut oil (or Bulletproof Brain Octane Oil; available online)

This is like a coffee version of butterbeer! If you are a coffee lover, try this clean and nutritious way of brewing coffee: the butter and coconut oil make it much easier on insulin and adrenal responses. Go easy on caffeine if you have overactive adrenals or suffer from panic attacks.

Brew the coffee with a mix of the hot and cold water. Pour the brewed coffee into a blender, add the butter and oil, and blend for 5 minutes, or until frothy.

Pour into glasses and drink immediately.

Aztec hot chocolate

Serves 2

¼ cup grated 100% raw unsweetened chocolate (cacao) or raw cocoa powder

½ teaspoon vanilla extract or the seeds of ½ vanilla pod

½ teaspoon ground cinnamon

Pinch of chile powder

Pinch of ground Szechuan pepper (optional)

1¼ cups boiling water or warm milk (any kind)

1 to 2 tablespoons raw honey or maple syrup

Raw cacao is rich in minerals, in particular magnesium and potassium. The buzz from the heat of the chile powder and Szechuan pepper aids circulation. The cinnamon helps to stimulate blood flow to cold extremities and the smell of the vanilla is enough to give your spirits a lift, so wrap your hands around a hot mug of goodness!

Combine the chocolate, vanilla, cinnamon, chile powder, and Szechuan pepper, if using, in a small saucepan. Slowly whisk in the water until the mixture is dark and a little frothy. Gently boil, whisking often, until thickened.

Sweeten with honey or maple syrup to taste, then pour into mugs and serve.

Brown rice horchata

This drink is a good option ahead of any endurance event such as a marathon. Try it daily in the week leading up to a marathon or any type of endurance event. It is rich in carbohydrates and minerals from the dates, and the cinnamon adds blood-sugar balancing effects, Add 2 teaspoons hemp protein powder for a nutrient-packed breakfast.

Serves 2

½ cup organic brown rice, rinsed (see Note)

1¼ cups almond milk or cow's milk (raw if you can find it)

Seeds from ½ vanilla pod or 1 teaspoon vanilla extract

½ teaspoon ground cinnamon, plus more for garnish

Pinch of sea salt

1 to 2 tablespoons maple syrup

Ice cubes

1 cinnamon stick

I used medium-grain brown rice, but short- and long-grain should work too. You can also use white rice.

Place the rice and 1¼ cups water in a container with a lid. Cover and refrigerate overnight.

Transfer the rice and water to a blender and blend until smooth. Strain the liquid through a muslin cloth or fine-mesh strainer, pushing on the solids to extract all the liquid.

Return the liquid to the blender and add the almond milk, vanilla, ground cinnamon, and salt. Blend until frothy, then blend in the maple syrup.

Serve over ice with a cinnamon stick garnish and a light dusting of ground cinnamon. The horchata will keep for 4 to 5 days in the fridge. Give it a quick stir before serving, as it has a tendency to separate.

Kombucha

This tangy, refreshing fermented drink is made from a SCOBY, also known as a symbiotic colony of bacteria and yeast. It helps create a harmonious internal microbiome—your gut flora—which is crucial for overall health. Go easy if you're not used to fermented foods or drinks—start slowly and build up and notice how you feel.

Makes 1 quart

4 tablespoons whole tea leaves or 3 tea bags (see Note)

6 tablespoons unrefined (raw if possible) superfine sugar

1 quart freshly boiled water

1 kombucha SCOBY (see page 92)

4 tablespoons brewed kombucha or raw apple cider vinegar

* You can use any kind of tea so long as it contains tannins, which provide food to keep the SCOBY going. Try white, green, oolong, Earl Grey, or a scented tea—jasmine is my favorite. You can also experiment with spices—try adding your favorite chai spices to black or oolong tea kombucha for a unique brew.

Place the tea leaves and sugar in a sterilized, heatproof 1½-quart glass jar. Let the water cool a little, then add it to the jar. Stir to dissolve the sugar and let it steep for 1 hour.

Strain the mixture into a new container, then return it to the original container and add the kombucha SCOBY. Cover the jar with a piece of cheesecloth or a thin, clean dishtowel. Secure with kitchen string or a rubber band and leave to ferment for 1 to 2 weeks. Taste after a week; you're aiming for a flavor that's a little yeasty but also a little tangy. The longer you ferment it, the sourer and less sweet it will taste. Pour into bottles and store in the fridge for up to 6 weeks.

After pouring your brew into bottles, store your SCOBY in a container at room temperature with about ¼ cup brewed kombucha, enough to cover it. It will keep for several weeks between brews.

FIZZY HANGOVER HELP
Brew kombucha as above, adding a few slices of fresh ginger with the tea, or add 1 teaspoon freshly grated ginger to 1 cup brewed kombucha. Infuse for 10 minutes, strain, then whisk in 1 teaspoon camu powder. It tastes—and fizzes—like Berocca and gives you a wonderful vitamin C boost.

Hibiscus cooler

Also known as "agua de jamaica," this popular drink is sold across Mexico, where an abundance of hibiscus plants line the roads. Hibiscus helps to ease coughs and colds and soothe sore throats. It's also useful for treating cystitis, soothing menstruation pain, and lowering blood pressure. Aim to drink two or three cups daily for acute conditions.

Makes 1 quart

5 tablespoons dried hibiscus flowers

1 quart freshly boiled water

2 to 4 tablespoons raw honey or maple syrup

Juice of 1 lime

Put the hibiscus flowers in a heatproof pitcher or container. Let the boiling water cool slightly, then add it to the pitcher along with 2 tablespoons honey. Infuse for at least 1 hour or, preferably, overnight in the fridge.

Strain the hibiscus flowers out. Add the lime juice, taste, and add more sweetener to taste. Drink cold.

Tepache

This popular fermented Mexican beverage is made from pineapple peel and rind, sweetened with piloncillo or brown sugar, seasoned with cinnamon, and served cold. Although it is fermented for several days, it contains very little alcohol.

Makes 1 quart

Peel of 1 pineapple (eat the fruit separately)

½ cup packed brown sugar or Mexican piloncillo

1 cinnamon stick

3 whole cloves

1 quart filtered or mineral water

Rinse the pineapple peel and finely chop it. Place it in a 1½-quart jar and add the brown sugar, cinnamon, cloves, and water. Cover with a piece of cheesecloth or a clean dishtowel and secure with kitchen string or a rubber band. Set aside in a cool, dark place to ferment for 24 hours.

Spoon off any white foam that has formed on the top. Cover again and leave for an additional 24 to 36 hours. Don't let it ferment longer, or you'll end up with pineapple vinegar.

Strain and serve, or pour into sterilized bottles and store in the fridge for up to 1 week.

Blood orange ginger beer

Making your own ginger beer is surprisingly easy and extremely satisfying. It takes a week to ferment, but hands-on prep time is only five minutes a day. Any seasonal fruit can be substituted for the blood oranges (rhubarb is amazing), or you can experiment with spices such as star anise, cinnamon, or cardamom. It's important to use organic ginger here because you are leaving the skin on (the skin contains beneficial bacteria and yeasts that encourage fermentation).

Makes about 1 quart

1 whole organic unpeeled fresh ginger root, approx. 4½ inches long

5 teaspoons unrefined sugar, plus ¾ cup

5 blood oranges

Turmeric Soda Variation
Replace the ginger with a 6-inch piece of fresh turmeric root and the blood oranges with the zest and juice of 2 lemons.

Grate 1 tablespoon of the ginger. In a 1-pint jar, combine with 1 teaspoon of the sugar, and 3 tablespoons filtered or mineral water. Cover with a piece of cheesecloth or a clean dishtowel, and leave to ferment in a cool, dark place for 24 hours, shaking it a couple of times.

Grate another tablespoon ginger into the mix and add 1 teaspoon sugar and 2 tablespoons water. Repeat daily for 5 days; at that point, you should start to see it fizz a little. This is your ginger bug.

On the sixth day, strip the zest from two of the oranges using a vegetable peeler. In a small saucepan, combine the zest with the juice from all the oranges with enough filtered or mineral water to bring the mix up to 1 quart. Add the remaining ¾ cup sugar. Bring to a simmer over medium heat, then reduce the heat and simmer for 15 minutes, or until the sugar has dissolved. Remove from the heat and cool completely.

Pour into a 1½-quart lidded jar. Add half of the ginger bug. Cover with a piece of cheesecloth or a clean dishtowel, and store in a cool, dark place, stirring once or twice daily. Top up the remainder of the ginger bug in the same way for future batches and store in the fridge between batches.

Taste the ginger beer daily, as it will continue to ferment and become less sweet. Once it is to your liking—generally 3 to 4 days—strain out the zest and pour into sterilized bottles. Let the bottles sit at room temperature for 1 to 2 days. "Burp" your bottles once or twice by opening then resealing them to release the pressure. Put your ginger beer in the refrigerator, and drink it within 2 weeks.

Jun tea

Thought to have originated in northern China and Tibet, jun is a probiotic drink made with green tea and honey. It's a light, effervescent, sweet, and slightly sour alternative to kombucha. If you're avoiding sugar, you may prefer it.

Makes 1 quart

1 quart filtered or mineral water

1 tablespoon green tea leaves (any variety)

3½ tablespoons raw honey

1 jun SCOBY (available online; see page 92)

⅓ cup jun tea from previous batch (comes with your SCOBY for your first brew)

In a large saucepan, bring the water to a boil. Add the tea leaves, remove from the heat. Steep for 30 minutes, then strain. Whisk in the honey until it dissolves.

Pour into a sterilized 2½-quart jar and add the jun SCOBY and tea from a previous batch. Cover the jar with a piece of cheesecloth or a clean dishtowel and secure with kitchen string or a rubber band. Set the jar on a plate to catch any liquid that may bubble over and place in a cool, dark place for 3 days.

Taste your jun; it should smell a little sweet and faintly sour. If you like the taste, bottle it up and make a new batch (see page 82 for caring for your SCOBY), or leave it for a few more days. The longer you ferment it, the more sour it will become. Bottle the jun in sterilized bottles and set out on the counter for 2 more days to get bubbly. As they are sitting, "burp" your bottles once or twice by opening then resealing them. This will release the pressure and prevent your bottles from exploding.

Store in the fridge until ready to drink. It will keep for 6 weeks or more.

Rye kvass

This traditional Slavic and Baltic brew is a healthy substitute for beer and a quick homebrew option with a very low alcohol content. It is nutritious, cooling, and energizing and an excellent digestive tonic. The molasses makes it rich in iron and acts as a blood builder.

Makes 1 quart

3½ ounces stale 100 percent rye sourdough bread

2 tablespoons molasses

2 tablespoons raisins or dried sour cherries, or ⅔ cup fresh blackberries

1 tablespoon active sourdough starter

1½ quarts filtered or mineral water, at room temperature

Whisk 3½ ounces strong bread flour with 3½ ounces warm water in a clean jar. Cover with a cloth and leave in a warm place for 1 day, stirring occasionally. Feed the mix with 3½ ounces flour and 3½ ounces cold water. When it bubbles and rises, it's ready to use.

Cut the bread into ¾-inch cubes. Make sure it is really dry. If not, dry it in a 200°F oven until hard but not burnt or toasted.

Put all the ingredients into a large jar (or evenly divide them between two jars), leaving at least 2 inches at the top. Cover with a piece of cheesecloth or a clean dishtowel and set in a cool, dark place away from direct sunlight to ferment for 2 to 4 days, until it becomes tangy and beerlike and bubbles start to form.

When you decide that the kvass is ready, put it in the fridge for a few hours or overnight. As it cools down, the sediments and bread solids will sink to the bottom of the jar. Strain the kvass carefully through cheesecloth, trying not to disturb the sediment at the bottom, and pour into sterilized bottles. The kvass can kept in the fridge for up to 1 week.

Moroccan mull

This is brimming with antioxidants, heart-healthy pomegranate and warming spices, and is a great alternative to mulled wine during the holidays. It's so aromatic and beautiful that my guests always choose it over mulled red wine. Pomegranate is thought to help clean the arteries and therefore have a cardiovascular protective action.

Makes 1 quart

1 quart pomegranate juice

1 tablespoon rose petals or
2 teaspoons rosewater

8 cardamom pods, crushed

2 star anise pods

2 cinnamon sticks

12 whole cloves

2 clementines, halved

Put all the ingredients into a large saucepan and bring to a simmer over medium-high heat. Reduce the heat and simmer for 15 minutes. Strain into heatproof glasses. For a richer flavor, steep the mixture in the fridge overnight and then rewarm it before serving.

My little black book

Get all you need to make the recipes throughout this book with these wonderful suppliers.

Canton Tea—an extensive range of organic loose leaf and herbal teas
www.cantonteaco.com

Mountain Rose—a one-stop online shop for organic dried herbs, flowers, spices, wheatgrass for sprouting, as well as brahmi, shatavari, beet and camu camu powders
www.mountainroseherbs.com

Soluna Garden Farm—another brilliant source for dried herbs, flowers, spiced and berries for making your own tea blends
www.solunagardenfarm.com

Yeomoos Nourishing Cultures—an online pitstop for kefir grains, kombucha scoby, sourdough starters and ginger beer plants
www.yemoos.com

Kombucha Kamp—for kombucha and jun tea scoby
www.kombuchakamp.com

dōTERRA—for a wide range of food grade essential oils
www.doterra.com

Drinks for...

Allergies and hay fever: *Lemon, lavender, and peppermint shot*

Anti-aging: *White tea, Green tea, Olive leaf tea, Citrus wake-up calls, Saffron and cardamom tea*

Arthritis: *Everyday health tonic, Golden chai, Turmeric shots, Olive leaf tea, Elderflower and lemon tea*

Bedtime: *Cozy bedtime tea, Sweet dreams tea*

Blood pressure and circulation: *Lime and cayenne shot, Aztec hot chocolate, Moroccan mull*

Breakfast: *Brain booster, Tropical detox smoothie, Golden chai, Golden lassi, Brown rice horchata*

Children: *Rosehip syrup, Golden lassi, Brown rice horchata, Hibiscus cooler*

Coffee addicts: *Brain booster, Chicory chai, Butter-froth coffee*

Coughs and sore throats: *Cough tonic, Bee balm vinegar, Elderflower vinegar, Elderflower and lemon tea*

Detoxing: *Dandelion and burdock cordial, Spiced dandelion tea, Celery and cilantro juice, Wheatgrass and gooseberry juice, Charcoal shot, Nettle and mint tea*

Digestion: *Zen tea, Mint vinegar, Pu-erh tea, Spice C tea, Rosy ginger tea*

Energy: *Vanilla and nutmeg matcha latte, Chlorella and coconut water, Jamu kunyit, Turmeric shots, Coconut milk*

Fighting colds: *Everyday health tonic, Garlic and lemon elixir, Thyme vinegar, Oregano vinegar, Tom yum tea*

Focus and concentration: *Brain booster, Rosemary vinegar, Grasshopper tea*

Gut Health (pro- and pre-biotic): *Water kefir, Milk kefir, Chicory chai, Sunflower seed milk, kombucha, Jun tea, Rye kvass*

Hangovers: *Wheatgrass and gooseberry juice, Fizzy hangover help*

Headaches and migraines: *Seasonal ginger shots, Lemon, lavender, and peppermint shot*

Immune boosting: *Elderberry syrup with echinacea, Rosehip syrup, Scarborough fair tea*

Iron boosting: *Nettle tonic, Beet kvass, Apple and parsley juice*

Menstrual cramps: *Lemon verbena and calendula tea, Women's balance tea, hibiscus cooler*

Parasites: *Celery and cilantro juice, Tropical detox smoothie, Pumpkin seed milk*

Relaxation and reducing anxiety: *Jasmine tea, Holy basil tea, Sweet dreams tea*

Upset tummies: *Seasonal ginger shots, Aloe cooler, Vietnamese lemongrass tea, Tummy soother*

Index

Index

Acknowledgments

Writing this book has made me realise just how much of my day is devoted to brewing and sipping things. It's been brilliant to have the opportunity to dote on my favorite infusions and bind them all together in this wonderful little tome.

Huge thanks to Judith Hannah and Kyle Cathie for thinking of me for this project. You're the wisest owls in the publishing world and it's been delightful working with you again. And, to Rebecca Sullivan for reconnecting us.

To the lovely Hannah Coughlin, thank you for pulling everything together, guiding the shoots, letting me slip in extra recipes at the umpteenth hour, and for really shaping this book.

This book would not be as beautiful and inspiring without photographer Ali Allen's stunning images, and Lucy Gowans' design skills. I could just pour over the gorgeous pages all day.

Eternal thanks to Edward Eisler from Jing Tea for opening the door to the wonderful world of tea. Your teas really are the finest and drinking them brightens my days. Enormous gratitude to Sally Gurteen for further adding to my tea knowledge.

Thank you to Sara Haglund for gifting me my first Scoby, which kickstarted many kombucha brewing adventures. To my friends and family, for trying all my weird and wonderful brews.

Last but not least, to Ciara Jean Roberts, who I've been seeing as a nutritional therapist for the past few years. You have poured a vast wealth of knowledge into this book. You have also taught me (and hopefully those of you who have bought this book) that simple, joyful, and delicious routines woven into your day can really make a dramatic difference to how you feel.